I AM NOT MISSING

Teresa Short Mitchell

Illustrated by Author's Tranquility Press

About the Author

PHILOSOPHY FOR LIFE

Mine is really simple. I ask for everything I want, need and desire. If I get it, then I am better off and it is a wonderful thing. If I do not, then I am no worse off than I was before I asked. (As an educator, I know that is a double negative). Basically, I believe my position can only improve.

PHILOSOPHY OF EDUCATION

Children are our future. We must plan and invest in our future. This means we must invest in children at an early age. The way I view it, we can invest in them with money, time, energy, understanding, love and education while they are young or continue to invest in more prisons, social dependency and societal fear as they grow older. Teresa Short Mitchell has served as an educator for thirty-two years. She holds a Bachelor's degree from Tuskegee University and a Master's and Specialist's degree from Troy State University. She has taught for the Pinellas County School District (Florida), Fort Benning and Clayton County Schools (Georgia) and served as an administrator for Harris County and Fulton County Schools. She has published a poetry book, Heartfelt Words: Words Speak When Hearts Cannot and the first book in a series, The Bathroom Tells on Me which was selected top 8 out of 15,000 books. Having served as a teacher, administrator, mother and grandmother, she has witnessed and helped others work through life and school-related issues. It is her goal to help as many caregivers as possible by publishing children books that provide insight and guidance. She currently lives in the Columbus, Georgia area.

Dedication

This book is dedicated to my granddaughter, Kayla who has no problem asking for everything she wants. It is written as a guide and resource for single parents, caregivers, foster parents, traditional, diverse and multiethnic families who share values such as building respect and accepting responsibility while spurring the imagination of children.

Key Vocabulary

buttering	gratification	immediate	participate	fetch
agreement	comparison	interrupted	frantically	perched
tremendous	veterinarian	approximately	encountered	binding
independent	trustworthy	approached	cautiously	witness
confidence	urgency	snuggled	glimpsed	retreat

Curriculum Standards

For educational purposes, this book supports the following skills/curriculum:

- Character feelings and emotions
- Cardinal Directions/Map Skills
- Drawing Conclusions
- Elapsed time
- Fiction and Nonfiction
- Inflectional endings
- Letter writing
- Parts of Speech
- Predicting outcomes
- Problem-solving
- Responsibility
- Self-esteem/Empathy
- Settings

Kayla is 12 years old, small in stature but within the normal size of a child her age with shoulder length straight black hair. Her heart and spirit are strong and they are her two best attributes. Some people call her Tiny. Her grandmother nicknamed her Pippy because most of the time, she wears her hair in two pony tails. You should read that story sometime soon.

Kayla, a free-spirited, independent child wanted her parents to give her more freedom, independence and responsibility so she had been buttering them up for weeks. One of her friends had gotten a new puppy for Christmas and she wanted one for her birthday. She had also grown tired of the afterschool program. During this time, she had been insisting that she was old enough to be at home alone for a little while. When she would ask her parents why she couldn't, they would navigate around her questions without answering yes or no.

Her birthday was right around the corner, so she wrote her parents a letter.

Dear Mom and Dad,

I will be 13 years old in a few days. That means I will finally be a teenager! I know I get on your nerves sometimes, but I am a good person, girl, student, and daughter.   Well, we get on each other's nerves (LOL). All I want for my birthday is my very own key to our house and my own puppy.

If I was writing this letter to Santa, I know he would bring them to me. Christmas is just so far away. I just can't wait that long. It is like you both say all the time, "You need immediate gratification." I also want to remind both of you how much you say you love me. Since you love me, could you show me how much?

Sincerely,

Your kind-hearted, independent daughter,
Kayla

P.S. Could you think about giving me a baby sister or brother for Christmas?

She placed the letter on the kitchen counter next to the stove and went to bed. The next morning at breakfast, she was so nervous. The letter was missing but her parents didn't mention it.

All day long, she wondered if they had read the note. She thought to herself, there was no wind so it couldn't blow away. She had quickly checked the kitchen floor and it hadn't fallen off the counter.

The bell rang signaling the end of the day. Her mother was there to pick her up. Thank goodness, she didn't have to stay in the afterschool program today.

As she buckled up, her mother said, "Your father and I got your letter." "Good," she said with a sigh of relief. "I worried if I should have sent an email with a read receipt." They both laughed. "It appears you are growing up. You took the time to carefully scribe your wishes for your birthday." Kayla's body began to tense up. Her mother continued, "You made a comparison of us to Santa Claus." "I'm sorry," she interrupted. "It's okay, your father and I have a surprise for you when we get home." Kayla's mouth dropped open. Before she could speak, her mother said, "Don't ask because I am not going to tell you."

When they arrived home, her father's car was in the driveway. She screamed, "Daddy's home!" The car had barely stopped when she opened the door, jumped out and ran into the house. "Where's the fire?" her mother humorously asked.

When she opened the front door, she saw her dad sitting at the kitchen table holding a white, fluffy animal that looked like a puppy. Kayla abruptly stopped in her tracks. She covered her face, took a deep breath and said, "Ooh." By this time, her mother had entered the house and was standing behind her. She gave her a gentle nudge and said, "Go ahead, she's yours." Kayla was so excited. She took the puppy and plopped down on the kitchen floor. Her heart was filled with joy and her eyes with tears. All of her worries went out the window. She had a puppy so she was in hog's heaven.

Kayla and her father went outside with her new puppy while her mother changed and prepared dinner. Her father said, let's sit down for a minute. Once sitting down, her dad asked, "Have you thought about a name?" "No." Her father continued, "You mean you thought about and wrote a detailed letter asking for a puppy and you never had a second thought about the name?" Kayla responded, "To be honest dad, I wasn't confident I would get it."

Her father recalled, there is an old saying, "Be careful what you ask for." Kayla looked a little confused. Her father began explaining that having a dog is a tremendous responsibility. It is one that she will share the brunt of accepting. She will feed, water, walk and bathe her puppy. When both of them are grown, she will still be responsible for feeding, watering, walking and bathing her dog. Then, he added, "Your mother and I will make sure she sees the veterinarian for her shots."

GD705

Kayla played with her puppy all weekend. She even fed, watered, walked and bathed Snow. When Monday rolled around, she didn't want to leave her new puppy. Her parents insisted. Her mother said, "You have been quite responsible for Snow this weekend. Your father and I think we will give you a chance to prove you can take care of Snow and yourself for a couple of hours after school." Kayla's face lit up. Her father added, "There are a few rules. Let's sit down and make sure we are all on the same page."

Her parents handed her a list and asked her to read each one out loud. Her mother said, after you read each one, we need you to explain what you believe it means.

I understand:

1. I MUST come straight home after school.

2. I must NOT allow anyone to visit while I am alone.

3. I must NOT open the door for anyone.

4. I must NOT leave the house until or unless my mother or father gives me permission. Exception: I can take Snow in the backyard since it is fenced.

5. I MUST feed Snow before I can take her in the backyard.

_______________________   _______________________
Print Name   Witness(es)

_______________________   _______________________
Signature

_______________________   _______________________
Date

"I can do this!" Her face and voice were filled with excitement. "Wait," her father said. "Since you are all independent and responsible, your mother and I need you to sign this agreement." "Sign?" Kayla asked. Her mother chimed in, "Yes, you wrote us a letter, we wrote you an agreement. We have given you everything you asked for before your birthday (handing her the house key)." Her father added, "Show that you love and respect us and that you will be responsible and trustworthy." "This is a binding agreement. Sign it or give back the key," her mother explained. Kayla signed the agreement and then her parents signed. That's when Kayla asked, "Can we go now?" She bent down, hugged and kissed Snow goodbye.

Monday was like reliving Friday except Kayla knew she had her puppy. All she could think about was Snow and how she would not have to stay in the afterschool program anymore. She was anxious to get home. The bell rang signaling the school day had ended. The bus stop was on the west side corner of her street. She was so excited when she stepped off the bus. She didn't even notice or hear her neighbor say hello as she was running home to see Snow.

When she opened her front door, Snow frantically greeted her. As Kayla bent down, Snow expressed her excitement by spraying the floor. "We better clean that up before mom and dad come home." She put her bookbag on the table in the family room, cleaned up Snow's accident and fed her.

Kayla sat down and began doing her homework while Snow snuggled next to her. "Whew, what's that smell? I better get you outside," Kayla said out loud. Kayla grabbed the leash and headed to the front door with Snow. She suddenly remembered her signed agreement with her parents, turned and went out the back door.

While they were in the backyard, Kayla and Snow were playing fetch and enjoying themselves. Kayla decided she would just let Snow run around while she finished her homework. It would be like killing two birds with one stone. She went inside, gathered her homework, returned to the patio, sat down and focused on her assignments. After a while, she didn't see Snow running anymore.

She called for her, but she didn't come. She walked around the backyard but didn't see her anywhere. She noticed the back gate was slightly cracked so she peeped out and called for Snow. When Snow didn't come, Kayla was forced to make a decision. She had to call her parents and appear not to be responsible on her very first day at home alone or leave the house without permission to find and bring Snow home before her parents arrived. She chose to go look for Snow. She looked down at her cell phone. It was 4:35pm.

Kayla knew she needed help. She didn't want the neighbors to tell her parents she was out looking for Snow, so she had to solicit help from the animals. She first encountered a frog. "Mr. Frog,' she asked, 'Did you see a small, white, fluffy puppy come this way?" "Ribbit," said the frog. "It went that way." "Thank you." Kayla headed east.

As she began walking, she saw a bluebird perched on a mailbox, so she stopped and asked, "Ms. Blue Bird, by any chance while flying about did you see a small, white, fluffy puppy?" "Chirp, chirp," responded Ms. Blue Bird. "Did you see which direction she went?" Ms. Blue Bird lifted her right wing and said, "She went that way." Kayla headed north.

After walking approximately two blocks, Kayla glimpsed a bunny near a hedge. "Hello, Mr. Bunny." Mr. Bunny yells out, "What's up, Doc?" Kayla inquires, "Have you seen a small, white fluffy puppy that looks like you?" Mr. Bunny takes ten bunny hops and tells Kayla to keep going in the same direction. Kayla thinks to herself that it is getting late. She checked the time on her cell phone. It was 5:00pm. Her mother will be arriving home soon. She feels a sense of urgency and must decide whether to keep searching for Snow or return home and face the music.

Kayla decides to continue looking for Snow. She is growing tired and walking very slowly. At that moment, she glimpsed a turtle out of the corner of her right eye. "Mr. Turtle, have you seen a small, white, fluffy puppy come this way?" "Snap, snap!" exclaims Mr. Turtle as he withdraws his head and neck from view. "Please Mr. Turtle, can you tell me which way she was going when you saw her?" Mr. Turtle's head reappears and he points his neck to the left. "Are you sure, Mr. Turtle? Mr. Bunny said she was headed this way," Kayla declares. Mr. Turtle's head retreats from sight.

It is decision time again. Kayla turned around and headed west. On the way back, she noticed the park. She had an idea. Maybe Snow had gone to the park to run and play. Kayla began walking through the park and calling Snow's name. As she walked by a pond, she saw a duck and asked, "Ms. Duck, by any chance, have you seen a small, white, fluffy puppy come this way in the past few minutes?" "Quack, quack!' 'Why are you asking me that?" "Well,' said Kayla, 'my mother and father bought me a puppy for my birthday. Today was my first day at home alone with her. I named her Snow. She ran away and I have to find her." Ms. Duck dips her head into the water and floats away.

Kayla is exhausted and decided to head home. After walking south approximately two blocks, she noticed a small alley way near one of the neighbor's homes. She checked the time. It was almost 6:00pm. She thinks to herself that this is her last chance to find Snow. She began calling Snow as she cautiously approached the alley. Snuggled against a fence near the back of the alley was Snow. She no longer looked fluffy and white. Kayla ran and picked her up. As she turned around, she saw her mother standing there. Her mother says nervously, "I was so worried. You were missing from the house so I came looking for you." Kayla explains, "I am not missing. Snow was missing. I went looking for her and I just found her." Her mother wraps her arms around Kayla and Snow as she says, "Let's go home."

Kayla's mother arrived home, found her asleep on the back patio, touched her left shoulder and said, "Kayla? Kayla, wake up!" Kayla looked up and saw Snow running around in the backyard.